©1987 SCOTT PUBLICATIONS
30595 EIGHT MILE, LIVONIA, MI 48152-1798
THIRD PRINTING
ISBN # 0-916809-19-6
PRINTED IN USA
No. 3504-6-93

How To Make

DOLL HATS 'N BONNETS

INTRODUCTION

Dolls are not a new craze or fad, they have been with us since the beginning of time in one form or another. All little girls and boys have enjoyed playing with dolls whether they were a crude cornhusk doll, one made of rags, carved in wood, or the finer porcelain models. Today's doll collector does include many varieties, but the most fashionable are those from the turn of the century period, made of porcelain and decorated in elaborate fabric costumes. An integral part of the dolls then, and for those reproductions being made today, is the decorative headwear. Hats and bonnets both were designed for dolls. This book includes designs, pictures and patterns for making hats and bonnets for your reproduction dolls to match those created by the original dollmakers. As you can see in the section of fine etchings that includes hats and ladies modeling hats, dolls of the period followed the style of women's fashions of the day. Use this book to make a variety of hats and bonnets by using the special patterns included in the two pull-out pattern sections. Each pattern was used to create a doll bonnet for a specific doll as shown in the illustrations. Sewing instructions are included with each pattern. We gratefully acknowledge the contribution by Helen B. Hansen of a special chapter on sewing headwear, and to Diana Anderson for supplying us with the illustrations from the 1879-1880 editions of the German publication, *Die Modenwelt*.

Headwear—Bonnets, Caps and Hats

There was a time when people didn't venture outside unless they had a covering on their head, and the many types and style of headgear would fill more than one book.

We will deal with just enough that our dolls will be well dressed and feel that their costumes are complete.

Baby bonnets can be simple or

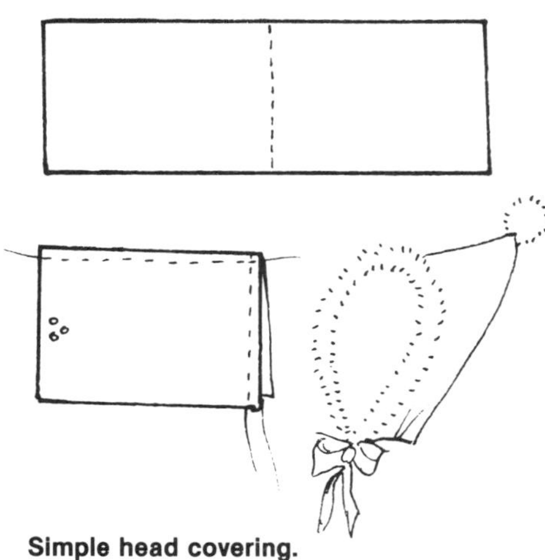

Simple head covering.

elaborate.

The simple one can be made of a rectangle piece of fabric long enough to fit around the baby's face and deep enough to come together at the back of her head. Sew a trim on one side of the rectangle piece and fold the material together lengthwise and stitch the back together. Sew a length of ribbon to bind the neck area and hold in any extra with tucks. Extend the ribbon for ties and turn the bonnet right side out. There will be a peak that can be trimmed with a tassel, a pom-pom or folded back and fastened down with a button for trim.

Another simple bonnet for a baby doll can be made from the same material as the dress or coat. Measure the doll over its head from below the ear on one side to below the ear on the

This chapter reprinted by special permission from the book "Custom Dressing Dolls" by Helen B. Hansen. "Custom Dressing Dolls" is also a Scott Publications Book.

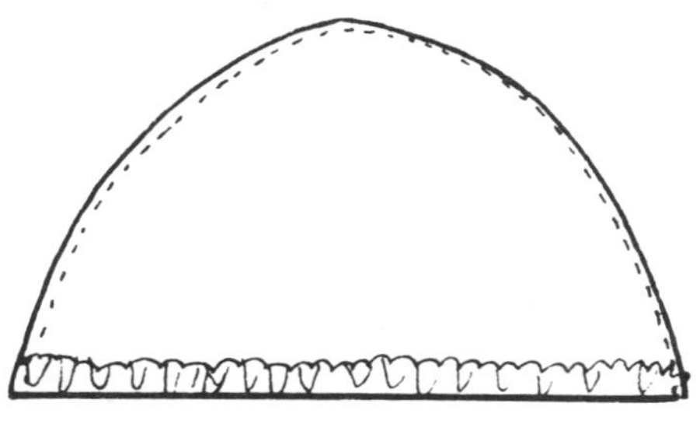

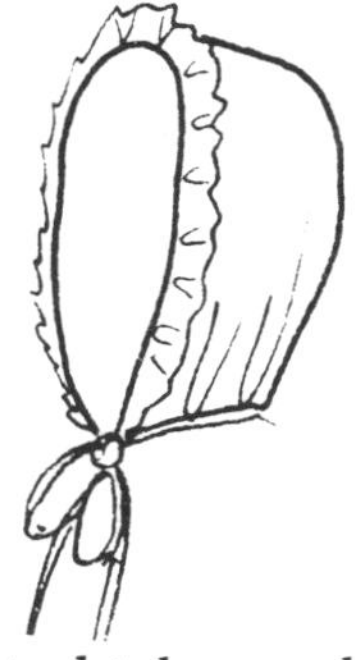

A very simple bonnet that can be made fancy with more trimming.

other. If the ear is high on the head, measure to where the side of the face joins the neck. Draw this line on a piece of paper and measure from the front center of the head over the crown to the nape of the neck. Draw this line perpendicular from the center of the first line and draw a half-circle from one end of the first line to the top of the second line

An attractive baby doll bonnet.

A "U" shaped piece in the back of the bonnet.

back down to the other end of the first line.

This simple bonnet has the rounded part gathered to fit the neck and can be trimmed in the front with a ruffle and lace.

Another style is a straight band of material over the head from ear area to ear area with an inset piece at the back, the shape of an upside-down U, that can have the open end pinched together a little if needed for a good fitting U.

This bonnet looks nice with gathered lace around the U and two rows across the front. A

A crocheted bonnet.

Another crocheted bonnet in the knot stitch.

The same type of doily shaped into a hat.

A crocheted doily made into a head covering.

Crocheted doily hat.

Dolly stiffened with sugar water.

Back view.

Front view.

A fancy bonnet.

Side view.

lace-edged ruffle can make it more elaborate. Again, try making a narrow band for the front piece and gathering a length of material between the front band and the inset at the back with gathered lace or a lace-edged ruffle between the first and second section of the bonnet. The silk bonnet that completes the costume on our K&R#122 is made in this style and, instead of a ruffle, has a poke that lays back over the front of the bonnet and is decorated with applique and trimmed in the same style as the coat.

Older dolls wear bonnets also, but they have pokes (a brim-like extension rounded to fit around the face) and are usually quite elaborate. The main body part of the bonnet is made with the U, a gathered stripe and a band. A poke over the face completes the bonnet and will need stiffening for it to hold its shape. I have used buckram, cardboard, plastic and multi-stitched rows on several layers of material.

If you want to add style, cut the gathered section wider through the center and eliminate the gathers down the straight side of the U.

Often, ribbons, flowers and feathers adorn these bonnets.

Another lovely bonnet can be made from a lace circle either crocheted with a simple stitch or an actual doily. A ribbon laced near the edge to fit the head and streamers with bows or ribbon rosettes over the ears, will complete this bonnet. The lace circle will also make a mop or beret-type of head covering. Small doilies, saturated with heavy sugar water and shaped over a cup or other shape with the edge pressed flat to a surface, will, when dry, make a lovely hat for a smaller doll.

I find buckram excellent for inner facing for the purpose of shape or body. I cut it the exact

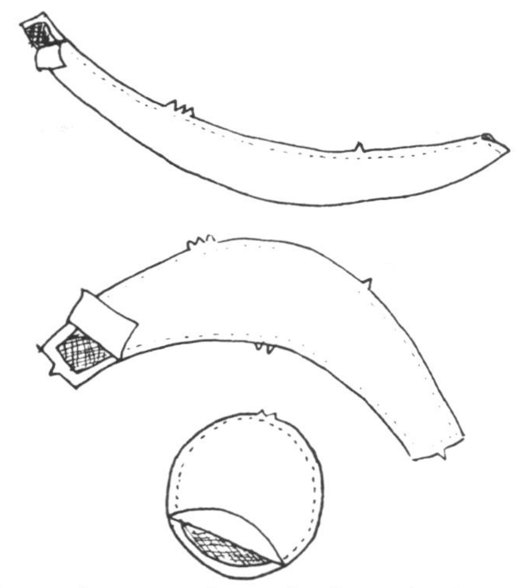

These diagrams show plastic or buckram inner lining that is enclosed within the hat and lining without being sewn in the seams.

size needed without a seam allowance and stitch it between two layers of the hat material. When the hat pieces are sewn together, you will have shape without bulk at the seams. For example: if I want a hat with a short crown, a flat top and a brim, I will make it with the enclosed buckram on the top and crown. The outside edge of the brim will not have a seam allowance but will be flush with the buckram and finished with a binding. If you want the brim to turn up slightly all around, pull the binding as you sew it to the brim. This will draw the brim in and cause it to turn up slightly.

Wire can be used to shape brims by enclosing wrapped milliners wire in the brims. There are several weights so use the one that works well with the material used and the style wanted. Use two strands of wire if one isn' strong enough.

Wire can be used to make shapes for lace or flower-covered bridal headpieces. A horsehair tubing can be purchased from a millinery supply house, which slips over the wire and provides a base on which to sew the lace or flowers. If you wish, lace can be glued to the wrapped wire but be sure the wire is wrapped in white if the lace is white.

The mop or dust cap is used for nightcaps, children's doll head covers and even fancy hats for older dolls. The basic pattern for a mop cap is a circle. An easy way to draw a circle is to make a loop at one end of a piece of string, decide on the size of the circle and make another loop in the string at the other end exactly half the size of the circle.

Place your pattern paper over a surface that you can put a thumb tack in, as one end of the string has a thumb tack to hold it in the center of the paper. Do not push the tack in all the way; let the string move freely. Place a pencil or pen point in the other loop and, holding the pen perpendicular, draw the circle with the string as the guide.

If you want a self-material ruffle, add the ruffle size. If the ruffle is to be lace or eyelet, no extra is needed. You will need to allow a casing for the elastic or drawstring needed to fit the cap around the doll's head.

This circle can be used for several other caps or hats. Sew the circle to a band that fits the

This is one version of a dust or mop cap.

One version of dust cap.

This tam is made by sewing the cutout darts.

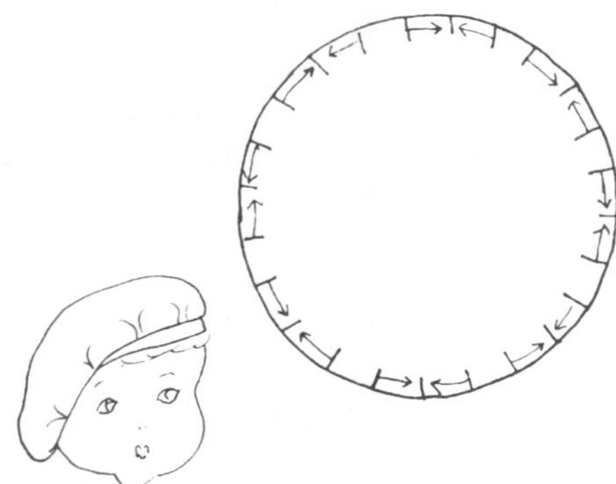

This tam is made by folding in box pleats and sewing the circle to a band.

doll's head and you have a boy's head covering. Add a small poke for a little older boy doll; or add a brim all around and you will have a lovely hat for any doll. Sometimes the brim can be a double straight or bias piece of the same material pleated or gathered. The possibilities are endless.

A boy's cap.

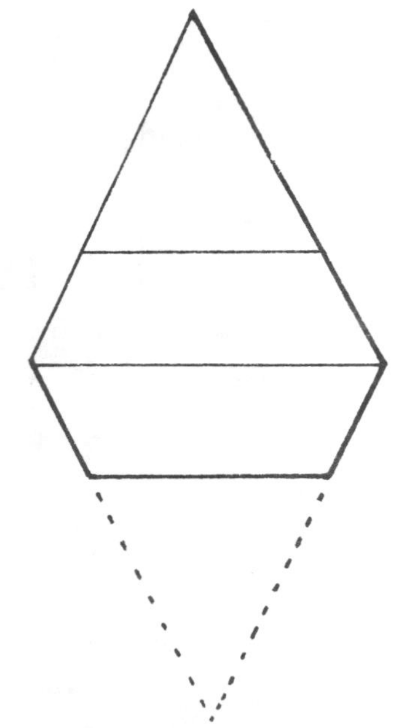

This is the A on a pattern for a pieced tam.

Another head covering is the boy's cap made with four or more pieces in the crown part and a visor-type brim across the front. This style can be adapted to a tam by cutting the pieces in an A shape on one side and extending the piece from the ends of the A legs in a reverse A shape ending at the crossbar of the A.

This tam is best when made with six or more sections. The total measurement of the crossbars will be the measurement around the doll's head.

Another tam can be made with two circles, one being doughnut shaped with the hole the size of the head's circumference.

The tam can also be made using a straight piece of fabric three times the measurement around the head and half the width of the desired finished size from one ear to the other. Allow for an elastic casing and gathering

A half bonnet using a poke and a band only.

Back view of a half bonnet.

rows.

To make this type, sew the two ends together and hem the casing. Sew the gathering rows on the other side and pull the threads tight as possible.

Sometimes, depending on the fabric, you cannot pull the threads tight enough to close the opening and you will have a hole. This hole can be covered with a circle of self-material and a pom-pom, or you can hand stitch the hole together from the wrong side. A tassel or two, a

A stitched brim hat.

Fancy poke bonnet.

Shaped with cardboard, back view.

A character hat.

Charming baby bonnet.

Baby bonnet with ruffle.

button or a loop of self-material can also be used for trim.

Commercial doll hats come in many styles and sizes, and most of them need trimming. Flowers and ribbons look nice and some brims look more finished if you bind them with material or ribbon. Even lace can be used for this purpose.

These hats make good foundations when you want a fabric-covered hat.

An easy, quick way to cover a hat with a brim is to cut a length of fabric the measurement around the outside of the brim

A fancy bonnet with knotted ribbon rosettes.

Side view.

Covered commercial hat with poke.

Back view.

Cloth covered straw hat.

Ribbon trimmed straw poke.

Back view.

Notice trim at poke edge.

and twice the depth of the brim plus seams. After sewing the ends together, stitch a gathering row on each side of the band and place the center around the edge of the brim with one gathered side to the underside and one on the top side. Pull the gathering threads to fit and hand stitch in place at the bend of the brim. Make a circle of material large enough to fit over the entire crown and stitch a gathering line around it. Hand stitch it in place and cover the raw edges with lace, ribbon or a band of self-material gathered through the center.

Try cutting the band for the brim and the trim around the crown on the bias. Often this gives a softer look. Sometimes it's necessary to use the fabric double so the weave of the commercial hat doesn't show through the fabric used to cover it.

A special hat can be made of felt or a man's old hat. This felt will need to be wet molded over a shape and dried.

One way for a doll to have a head covering to complete her costume but still show her beautiful hair is to sew a poke to a band, attach ribbons at each end of the band and tie under chin.

Pattern Sections 1 and 2

The hats and bonnets presented in our two pull-out pattern sections offer a variety of styles to costume your dolls. Following are brief descriptions and measurements for the hats/bonnets. Please keep in mind that the head sizes may vary if the dolls are wearing wigs.

Section 1

Boy's Cap
13" doll, 9" head

Bye Lo Cap
17" doll, 15" head

Bunting Cap
13" doll, 9" head

Bonnet with Ruffles and Lace
18" doll, 10"-11" head

Bonnet with Lace Brim
26" doll, 14" head

Section 2

Flapper Hat
16" doll, 7" head

Bonnet with Feathers
22" doll, 12"-13" head

Pillbox
23" doll, 14" head

Bonnet
13" doll, 8"-9" head

Cap for Petite Doll
12" doll, 6"-7" head

Bonnet with Lace and Flowers
19" doll, 11" head

Bonnet for Googly
10" doll, 8" head

Bonnet for Hilda
19" doll, 14" head

Pull-Out Hat/Bonnet

Pattern Section

The pattern sections in this book are unique in that they are designed to be removed from the book and used. The patterns are printed on quality paper and contain full sewing instructions for each pattern. The patterns are printed on only one side of the paper so that you will not find it necessary to trace patterns before cutting the fabric.

Although you may cut patterns directly out of each section, we recommend that you trace them onto another sheet of paper when using the pattern pieces for cutting fabric. Using the traced pattern will preserve the patterns in each of these pattern sections for future dolls you may want to make. *We also suggest that you make a trial pattern from large, soft thick paper towels to assure proper fit. This will also allow you to cut the fabric with greater accuracy.*

To remove the pattern sections from the book, carefully open the staples to lift out the attached section then bend the staples shut to keep the book intact.

Designs of the Times

Women were seldom seen without some type of hat or bonnet at the turn of the century. This head covering ranged from scarves on the simple side to elaborate bonnets designed after, copied from, or were actual European creations. These hats and bonnets were a necessity for little girls, too, so logically their dolls had to have them also. This section of the book is a collection of bonnets and hat designs selected from the late 1800's. These actual hats and bonnets were worn by young and old, rich and poor. By browsing through these illustrations, you will find you can get many ideas on how to dress your doll with a hat or bonnet. The important part of this section is that by examining each illustration you will be able to create your own original hat design. Simply select various elements of hat design from the wide variety offered here and put them together. We think that your imagination will run wild with all the creations you find possible. If you simply want to copy an idea, do that, or better yet; take some elements of those pictured on the following pages and incorporate them into the patterns provided in the two pull-out sections.

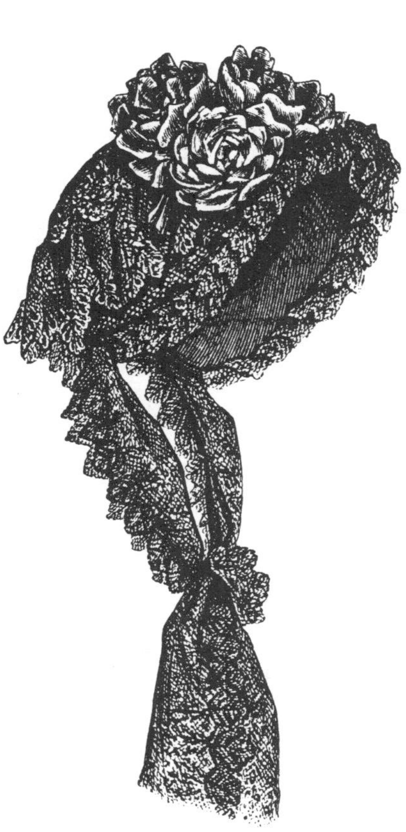